NOTORIOUS AMERICANS AND THEIR TIMES

Bugsy
SIEGEL
and the Postwar Boom

by

STEVE OTFINOSKI

BLACKBIRCH PRESS, INC.
WOODBRIDGE, CONNECTICUT

Published by Blackbirch Press, Inc.
260 Amity Road
Woodbridge, CT 06525

e-mail: staff@blackbirch.com
Web site: www.blackbirch.com

©2000 by Blackbirch Press, Inc.
First Edition

Printed in China

10 9 8 7 6 5 4 3 2 1

Library of Congress Cataloging-in-Publication Data
Otfinoski, Steven.
Bugsy Siegel and the postwar boom / by Steven Otfinoski.
     p.   cm. — (Notorious Americans and their times)
   Includes index.
   Summary: A biography of the infamous gangster and murderer who
was responsible for the building of the Flamingo hotel in Las Vegas.
   ISBN 1-56711-224-2 (hard: alk. paper)
   1. Siegel, Bugsy, 1906–1947—Juvenile literature. 2. Criminals
(U.S.)—Biography—Juvenile literature. 3. Outlaws—West (U.S.)—
Biography—Juvenile literature. [1.Siegel, Bugsy, 1906-1947.
2. Criminals.] I. Title. II. Series.
HV6248.S5619 O84 2000
364.1'092—dc21   00-009074
                                                     CIP
                                                     AC

Table of Contents

Chapter 1

GROWING UP IN THE GANGS
THE EARLY YEARS

*I*n 1997, the Hilton hotel chain celebrated the 50th anniversary of the first casino and hotel on the legendary Las Vegas strip, the Flamingo, which it had bought in 1971. It was a gala event, but amid all the celebrating, something was missing. No mention was made of the man who had actually built the Flamingo and whose vision had turned Las Vegas from a dusty, cowboy town to the gambling and

Opposite: Notorious gangster Bugsy Siegel was responsible for having one of the most extravagant casinos built on the Las Vegas strip.

entertainment capital of the world. The seemingly forgotten man was Benjamin "Bugsy" Siegel.

When questioned about the omission, a Hilton spokesperson replied, "The Bugsy image was not something that was particularly endearing to the Flamingo or Hilton....We're talking about a robber, rapist, and murderer. Those are not endearing qualities."

Bugsy Siegel was certainly all these things. And yet, while alive, he did endear himself to many people, even the glamorous stars and starlets of Hollywood, where he spent the last decade of his life. Of all the gangsters of the 20th century, Bugsy Siegel remains one of the most colorful and intriguing. Like Al Capone and John Dillinger, he captured the imaginations of Americans. But his was not a happy life. Siegel's life is a grim reflection of the dark side of the American Dream—one man's desperate and ruthless search for success, wealth, fame, and respect.

The American Melting Pot

It's a long way from the casinos of Las Vegas to the streets of Williamsburg, New York, where Benjamin Siegelbaum was born on February 28, 1906. Young

Hundreds of thousands of European immigrants came through Ellis Island when they arrived in the United States in the 1900s.

Benjamin's parents were two of the hundreds of thousands of immigrants who had come from Europe looking for a better life in America. Many of these immigrants—especially those from northern Europe—headed west to settle down and farm on the rich fertile land of the Midwest, which was much like the land they had left behind. Other immigrants—many of them from southern and central Europe—stayed in New York City, where they first arrived. Many of these people were experienced artisans and manual laborers who wanted to use their skills in America's biggest city.

By 1900, one-third of New York City's population was foreign born. According to famed journalist Jacob Riis, "a map of the city, colored to designate nationalities, would show more stripes than on the skin of a zebra, and more colors than any rainbow."

Williamsburg, a section of Brooklyn, New York, was home to three major ethnic groups—the Irish, Italians, and Jews. Ben Siegelbaum's family were Russian Jews who had fled persecution from the Czar (Russian king). Ben's father was a laborer who worked long hours for little pay. The elder Siegelbaum could barely support his wife and five children. From an early age, Ben, the blue-eyed, slender boy, vowed he would do anything to rise out of the poverty of his childhood.

This was easier said than done. Immigrant children were poor, uneducated, and had few opportunities to improve themselves. Some followed their parents into factory jobs, where they made only a meager living. Others, with more ambition and talent, tried their luck in the entertainment business or even pursued an education. A few chose a quicker but more dangerous path to success—crime. Ben Siegel, as he called himself, decided to follow the path of crime.

Apprenticeship in Crime

Crime and violence existed all around the children growing up in the crowded tenements of America's cities in the early 1900s. Getting "beat up" by a bigger kid on the street was a daily threat. You had to fight back or become a victim. Many slum children joined gangs to give themselves a sense of identity and power. These gangs stole and got involved in other street crimes. Most of their victims were other slum dwellers. Many immigrants had a fear of the

Many children in New York lived in crowded tenements like these.

police and authorities, a carryover from their experiences with corrupt and hostile governments in Europe. This natural fear made immigrants easy prey for the gangs.

One of the most common victims were pushcart peddlers. These peddlers were unskilled workers who rented a cart for a dime a day and sold wares on the city streets. They peddled everything from fruits and vegetables to used clothing. Young Ben Siegel and his friend Moe Sedway got their start in crime by taking "protection" money from Williamsburg's pushcart peddlers. First, they would ask a pushcart owner for money. When he refused, they poured kerosene on his cart and set it on fire.

Pushcart peddlers lived on the crowded streets of downtown New York City.

Next time, the owner would readily give them the money. In return, Ben and Moe would see that no other young "toughs" bothered the peddler—as long as he regularly paid them the "protection" money.

George and Meyer

Around this time, Benny made two more lifetime friendships.

One friendship was with George Ranft, who was as tough and wild as Benny. The two got into constant scrapes with the police. But as they grew older, Ranft decided to pursue another path. He used his talent and ambition to get a job dancing with a female partner in a nightclub. From there, Ranft got a part in a Broadway show. Eventually, he changed his name to George Raft and moved to Hollywood to act in movies.

Benny's other best friend was another child of Jewish immigrants, Maier Suchowlyindo, who changed his name to Meyer Lansky. When Ben met him, Lansky was an apprentice in a tool-and-die factory. But, like Ben, he had bigger ambitions. Lansky wanted to be a big-time gambler. The two young men shared similar goals, but they had very different

Meyer Lansky (left) was one of Bugsy Siegel's closest friends, as well as a "business partner."

personalities. Ben was wild, impulsive, and carefree. Lansky, who was six years older, was quiet, cautious, and thoughtful. They became the best of friends despite these differences. Ben watched out for Lansky, and Lansky treated Ben like a younger brother. He called him "little Benny" and made him his number two man. Together, they formed their own gang: Lansky was the boss and brains, and Ben provided the muscle.

Ben's unpredictable behavior earned him the curious nickname of "Bugsy." In gangster lingo, a gang member who was "bugsy" was a little "crazy" in the head. While the nickname was meant as a mark of respect among mobsters, Ben hated it. One sure way to see Bugsy Siegel go "bugsy" was to call him Bugsy to his face. More than one person found that out—the hard way.

"Bugsy never hesitated when danger threatened," recalled "Doc" Stacher, another member of the so-called Bugs and Meyer Gang. "While we tried to figure out what the best move was, Bugsy was already shooting. When it came to action, there was no one better. I've never known a man who had more guts."

The Bugs and Meyer Gang

The Bugs and Meyer Gang was just one of many criminal gangs operating on the Lower East Side of Manhattan, in a neighborhood appropriately named "Hell's Kitchen." Among the other members of this gang of young Jewish hoods was Meyer's brother, Jake; Lepke Buchalter, later head of New York's powerful crime gang, Murder, Inc; and a young man named Arthur Flegenheimer, who would soon change his name to Dutch Schultz. The gang quickly graduated from running dice games to participating in robberies, burglaries, and car thefts. They competed with the Italian gangs, who were part of the organized Italian crime family known as the Mafia. The most ambitious of the young Italian gang leaders was a cocky, young fellow named Charley Luciano.

One day, Luciano's gang met up with Lansky, who was alone. Although he was outnumbered, Lansky stood up to the Italian toughs. Luciano admired the guts of this feisty little thug, whose nickname was "Little Man." Soon they became the best of friends. Such a friendship in the crime world was almost unheard of. Criminals from different ethnic groups mistrusted each other, and nearly all of them were suspicious of the Jews. The older Italian mob bosses were suspicious of everyone—even other Italian mob leaders. They ran their own crime empires with a constant fear of being "taken out" or betrayed from within. But Luciano and Lansky were a new breed of criminal. They saw that cooperation and organization worked better than fighting.

These young gang members, however, could be just as brutal as their elders when they were crossed. When Luciano went to prison on a drug charge, he swore revenge on the Brooklyn cop's son who had "set him up." Lansky and Siegel agreed to help their friend. After he finished his six-month sentence, they told Luciano to go out of town. They wanted to be sure Luciano had an alibi. Then Lansky and Siegel killed the cop's son. This may have been young Ben's first murder. It would certainly not be his last.

Prohibition

Crime was a major issue that concerned Americans, especially in big cities. But of equal concern to many people was the consumption of alcohol. By the second decade of the 20th century, Americans were drinking more alcohol than ever before, worsening a

Police tried to close many of the illegal breweries that were banned during Prohibition.

GROWING UP IN THE GANGS: THE EARLY YEARS

The Triangle Shirtwaist Factory Fire

Immigrants who were too honest to turn to crime but not educated or skilled enough to get a good job, were often forced to work in crowded, filthy factories called "sweatshops" on New York's Lower East Side. Sweatshops were factories—often no more than tenement buildings—that had little ventilation and were unbearably hot. With heavy dangerous machines, often toxic raw materials, and young children as workers, sweatshops were disasters that were waiting to happen. On March 25, 1911, one disaster became real.

Sweatshops were often run with child labor.

It was about closing time on a Saturday afternoon, and the hundreds of teenage girls working at the Triangle Shirtwaist Company were eager to get off work and enjoy the evening. At first, no one noticed when a small fire broke out in a bin of fabric scraps on the eighth floor of the building. By the time someone did see the fire, it had spread, fueled by piles of material on the cutting tables.

The panicked workers rushed to escape from the rising flames. Some ran to the elevators to escape. Only one elevator was

The Triangle Shirtwaist company fire led to at least 145 deaths.

working, and that was soon jammed by the bodies of girls who had jumped into the elevator shaft. Other workers broke through the locked doors to the staircase. Still others headed for the flimsy fire escape, which collapsed under the weight of all the fleeing women. Trapped by the fire, more than forty girls leaped to their deaths from windows. Some were assisted by a young man. "He saw that a terrible death awaited them in the fire," wrote one reporter at the scene, "and his was only a terrible charity."

When the fire was over, at least 145 workers were dead. Some 100,000 mourners attended the mass funeral. Many New Yorkers blamed the tragedy on the neglect of the owners and a lack of regulations from the city. The court system, which favored the upper-class owners, cleared them of all charges. Nevertheless, the Triangle Shirtwaist Fire—one of the worst disasters in the city's history—led to important reforms in building safety, worker safety, and fire prevention.

variety of social problems. More and more workers missed work because they were drunk. More husbands beat their wives when they drank, and many fathers who drank too much neglected their children. The temperance (anti-drinking) movement got a big boost with the coming of World War I (1914-1918). When the United States entered the war in 1917, grain was needed to feed the armed forces. Prohibitionists argued that using grain to make alcohol was unpatriotic and that the only way to end this use was to ban the manufacture and sale of alcohol altogether. The majority of Americans were convinced by this argument. In 1917, Congress passed the Eighteenth Amendment to the Constitution, which prohibited the export, import, manufacture, sale, and transporting of all alcoholic beverages in the United States. It took another year for three-quarters of the states to approve the Prohibition amendment and make it law. Then Congress passed the Volstead Act in 1919 to provide penalties for anyone who violated Prohibition.

But Prohibition created far more problems than it solved. Small-time criminals across America saw an opportunity to provide alcohol illegally to the nation's drinkers. Since prohibition didn't exist in Canada, the Bugs and Meyer Gang helped to transport Canadian whiskey within the United States. They also weren't above hijacking the shipments of rival gangs. Overnight, many small-time operations, such as the Bugs and Meyer Gang, found themselves making incredible amounts of money selling "bootlegged" (illegally manufactured) alcohol.

The more money the gangs made, the more greedy they became. They began to fight over territory for their bootlegging operations. Cities like Chicago and New York became the scenes of bloody shoot-outs between rival gangs. The Roaring Twenties had arrived, and much of their "roar" was the sound from submachine guns rattling in the hands of gangsters.

Chapter 2

THE TWENTIES ROAR
MOVING UPTOWN

Class, that's the only thing that counts in life," Bugsy Siegel used to tell his friends. "Class. Without class and style a man's a bum, he might as well be dead."

Siegel believed these words and he lived by them. Earning close to a million dollars from his gang's wholesale liquor business, Siegel lived life to the hilt. He dressed in the best clothes money could buy, wore a snap-brim hat, and bought an expensive house in Scarsdale—an exclusive suburb of New York—for his wife Esta and their two daughters. He himself lived a good part of the time in a suite at New York's finest hotel, the Waldorf-Astoria, two floors below his friend Charley Luciano.

Few gangsters of the day sought the limelight as intensely as Bugsy Siegel. He made friends with actors and journalists, such as columnist Mark Hellinger. He was often seen in public at Broadway shows and nightclubs.

While Siegel was enjoying life, Meyer Lansky was keeping track of the gang's investments. He ran the gang's criminal activities like a Wall Street account-ant. The Italian godfathers, however, resented this "upstart Jew." Luciano received pressure from his boss, New York Mafia chief Joe Masseria, to stop deal-ing with Lansky and his gang, but Luciano wouldn't listen. If the old-time Italian gangsters didn't like these young hoodlums, others recognized their abilities. "If they [Luciano and Lansky] had become president and vice president of the United States," declared one Luciano gang member, "they would have run the place far better than the idiot politicians that did it."

Harding and The Teapot Dome Scandal

Certainly, the politicians could have learned a thing or two from the smooth operation of the Lansky-Luciano gang. Warren Harding, elected president in 1920, was a handsome, good-natured senator from Ohio. Harding, a man of mediocre abilities, was out of his depth as president—something he himself recognized. Once he confided to his secretary, "I don't know what to do or where to turn....Somewhere there must be a book that tells all about it....But I don't know where that book is, and maybe I couldn't read it if I found it!"

To boost his confidence, Harding surrounded himself with old cronies from back home in Ohio. Some of these men took advantage of their closeness to the president to make money through bribery and corruption. News of corruption in the Harding administration first surfaced in 1923. The president felt hurt and betrayed by his friends, and the stress probably contributed to the heart attack that led to his death in August of that year. Within months of Harding's death, the scandals became public.

The most publicized scandal involved Harding's Secretary of the Interior, Albert B. Fall. Fall had put all

Scandals, such as Teapot Dome, cast a cloud over Warren Harding's presidency.

Calvin Coolidge became president in 1923, after Warren Harding died.

of the U.S. naval reserved oil fields under the control of his department. Then he leased two of the reserves—Teapot Dome and Elk Hill—to two oil companies, that just happened to be run by two of his friends. Fall, the investigation uncovered, had sold the government oil reserves for almost $400,000 and a herd of cattle for his ranch in New Mexico. He was eventually convicted of accepting bribes and was sentenced to a year in jail and a $100,000 fine. What came to be called Teapot Dome was one of the worst scandals in American political history.

To put the upsetting past behind them, Americans turned to the new president, Calvin Coolidge, who had been vice president under Harding. Coolidge was a humorless but honest New Englander and had a reputation as a man of few words. When a woman sitting next to him at dinner said she had made a bet with a friend that she could get more than two words out of him in conversation, Coolidge is said to have replied, "You lose."

As a conservative Republican, Coolidge believed the least government was the best government. "The business of America," he once said, "is business." He left business to grow on its own without any interference or control from government.

The Stock Market Crash

Economic growth caused people to become overly optimistic, which caused the stock market to soar. More and more Americans invested their savings in the stock market, hoping to get rich quick. A large number of stocks were bought and sold many times each day, pushing them far beyond their actual worth. Many investors bought stocks on margin, or credit. This meant that a large portion of the wealth on Wall Street was not backed by actual money, only the promises to pay that money. With every day that went by, the stock market was pushed closer and closer to disaster. Finally, in late October 1929, the stock market collapsed.

"The streets were crammed with a mixed crowd," wrote journalist Elliott V. Bell, who was on Wall Street that terrible day. "Agonized little speculators, walking aimlessly...sold-out traders morbidly impelled to visit the scene of their ruin; inquisitive (curious) individuals and tourists, seeking by gazing at the exteriors of the [Stock] Exchange and the big banks to get a closer view of the national catastrophe..."

Many stockholders lost everything they had in the Crash of '29. During the economic depression that followed, companies and factories across America went out of business. Soon, 12 million Americans found themselves out of work.

A Gangland Struggle for Power

A few weeks before the Crash, Charley Luciano met with rival Mafia boss Salvatore Maranzano on New York's Staten Island. Luciano wanted to make peace, but the meeting did not go as he had expected it

During the Depression, unemployed Americans lined up at soup kitchens for food.

would. Maranzano ordered Luciano to end his relationship with Lansky. He told Luciano he wanted him to work for him instead. He also wanted Luciano to kill Joe Masseria, Luciano's official "employer." Masseria, the most reactionary of the Italian bosses, stood in the way of the united Mafia that Maranzano was trying to establish in New York. To drive home his point to the younger gangster, Maranzano had his goons beat Luciano and slash his face with a knife.

When Lansky found his partner, Luciano was half dead. He recovered, however, which earned him the nickname of "Lucky."

Luciano and Lansky vowed vengeance on Maranzano, but they knew they had to be patient. To take on that kind of power, they needed a lot more strength. In the meantime, they would eliminate Masseria, who was an obstacle to both of them and to Maranzano. In April 1931, Luciano invited Masseria to have dinner at a restaurant on Coney Island. Before the meal ended, Luciano excused himself and went to the restroom. Bugsy Siegel and three other gunmen entered the restaurant and riddled Masseria with a barrage of bullets.

Maranzano, of course, was pleased by this turn of events. He appointed Luciano his top lieutenant. But Luciano and his Jewish partners had other plans. About five months after Masseria's death, four neatly dressed men claiming to be from the IRS (Internal Revenue Service) entered Maranzano's office to "check his business records." It was too late by the time the "boss of all bosses" realized that the men had been sent by Lansky and Luciano. They tied Maranzano to a chair and killed him.

Birth of the Syndicate

With Masseria and Maranzano gone, the old era of organized crime in America came to an end. Lansky and Luciano were now free to join the various gangs together into a well-run crime machine that would come to be called the "Syndicate." They saw the constant fighting between one gang and another as counterproductive, and hoped it would also become a thing of the past.

The Syndicate couldn't have been organized at a better time. In 1933, after 13 years, the Prohibition Amendment was widely viewed as a failure and was repealed (withdrawn). Because alcoholic beverages could again be sold legally, bootleggers were now out of business. The Syndicate had to look to other ways to make money. They put all their efforts into illegal gambling, prostitution, and narcotics (drugs). But the most profitable growth industry for the Syndicate was providing the service of murder. Mob bosses organized a separate branch to deal exclusively with killing people who stepped out of line or committed some "crime" against the Syndicate. The organization was called Murder, Inc., and one of its founders was Bugsy Siegel.

~ MURDER, INC. ~

"We only kill each other," Bugsy Siegel once assured a friend who wasn't a part of organized crime. These words could have been the slogan for Murder, Inc., the branch of the Syndicate that Lansky, Siegel, and other gang leaders formed in the early 1930s. To kill a cop or a reporter would have brought the full force of the police down on the Syndicate and that could have hurt business. Killing rival gangsters, stool pigeons (informers), and other "family" members who strayed would not arouse as much public outcry or concern.

Exactly how many people were killed by Murder, Inc. is unknown. Some crime experts claim as many as 1,000 gangsters met their deaths at the hands of this organization. Like everything else in the Syndicate, Murder, Inc. was run like a business. After careful planning, a contract was put out on a person anywhere in the country, professional killers were sent to the scene, and the "rub-out" was accomplished.

The "employees" of Murder, Inc. were a ghoulish gallery of blooded killers. Abe "Kid Twist" Reles was the top lieutenant of the group, until he was arrested and turned "stool pigeon." Frank "The Dash" Abbandando got his nickname after he dashed past one victim, ran around the block, and finished the "hit" from behind. Harry "Pittsburgh Phil" Strauss was probably the coldest killer of them all. It was said that he rarely even knew who he was killing—he wouldn't know their names until he read the morning's newspaper.

The Heat Is On

Murder, Inc. made killing into a business. For Siegel, however, killing was often personal as well. One day in 1934, a bomb was dropped down the chimney of the gang's headquarters in New York. Rival gangster Tony Fabrizzo was responsible for the sabotage, and Siegel swore revenge.

To set up a perfect alibi, Siegel checked himself into a hospital for treatment of a supposed nervous breakdown. One night, he sneaked out of his hospital room, and met up with other gang members. They paid a visit to Tony Fabrizzo and shot him dead. Siegel returned to his hospital room and climbed back into bed, with no one the wiser.

The public was becoming increasingly outraged by the growing wave of crime and violence. During Prohibition, many people had seen gangsters in a sympathetic light, breaking laws that many people felt were unfair. Now that Prohibition had ended, Americans saw organized crime in a far less favorable light. The public's new champion was crusading New York State Attorney Thomas E. Dewey. In 1935, the governor of New York appointed Dewey as the special prosecutor for vice and rackets in New York

City. In this role, Dewey worked tirelessly to prosecute and convict gangsters in the Syndicate.

In 1936, Dewey got a warrant to arrest Lucky Luciano for operating a prostitution ring. Luciano fled to Arkansas but was brought back to New York by law officers. He was tried, convicted, and sentenced to 30 to 50 years in prison, an unheard-of sentence for a top crime boss. Before starting his sentence, Luciano turned over all his financial affairs to Meyer Lansky, who in effect became the head of the Syndicate.

Bugsy Siegel was on Dewey's list as well, and his alibi for the Fabrizzo killing was beginning to crumble. Siegel's love of publicity was making him vulnerable, and he knew it would only be a matter of time before he was arrested.

Leaders in the Syndicate had two choices. They could put Siegel "to sleep" so he wouldn't bring the pressure on others, or they could get him out of town. Lansky and Siegel convinced the other bosses to choose the second option. The West Coast had the potential to be big business, and it was a region the Mob wanted to cultivate. Siegel was sent out to California to help organize the rackets and turn them

New York State Attorney Thomas E. Dewey was a crusader against organized crime.

THE TWENTIES ROAR: MOVING UPTOWN

into a new profit center. He was happy to leave New York—and not just because he was in danger if he stayed there. "As time went on Bugsy became a little restless at always being second fiddle to Meyer," said gang member Doc Stacher. In California, Bugsy would have a new kind of independence—a free hand to build a crime empire of his own. He knew this was his chance to show the bosses that he, too, was truly "boss" material. It was a golden opportunity that he intended to make the most of.

Chapter 3

THE HOLLYWOOD DREAM FACTORY
BUGSY GOES WEST

*W*hen Bugsy Siegel arrived in California in 1937, Hollywood was in its "golden age," turning out hundreds of movies each year.

Movie Capital of the World

Hollywood's story began 54 years earlier in 1883, when Kansas businessman Harvey Henderson Wilcox bought a 120-acre ranch in what was then known as Cahuenga Valley. He cut it up into tracts for expensive homes. His wife changed its name to Hollywood, because she thought it sounded quaintly English. The Wilcoxes were prohibitionists and in 1901, they banned alcohol from their community. Ironically, ten years later, this ban led to the birth of Hollywood's movie industry.

A movie crew from Nestor Studios in New York was looking for a location to make movies in the winter.

Founded by Harvey Henderson Wilcox in the 1880s, Hollywood became the home of the nation's movie industry.

Hollywood's one public drinking place closed down, and the crew turned the building into an indoor studio. Soon other Eastern studios were attracted to Hollywood's sunny climate and excellent exterior locations. This little residential community would never be the same.

With the coming of sound films, or "talkies," in the late 1920s, Hollywood's reputation grew. While most American businesses were in a slump during the Depression years of the 1930s, the movie industry was booming. Most Americans may have had little money to spend on entertainment, but nearly everyone could afford the 25-cent admission price to the movies once a week. Hollywood, called by some "the dream factory," provided the kind of escapist entertainment that millions of Americans needed during those grim years. For their 25 cents, patrons got to see two feature-length movies, a cartoon, a newsreel (documentary film about the news of the day), and previews of coming attractions.

The movie houses were a show in themselves. Just about every city had its own movie "palace," most of them built in the 1920s. Each palace had its own architectural style and theme, ranging from an

The Roxy Theatre, in New York City, was one of the nation's most popular movie houses.

Italian garden to an Oriental palace. One of the most extravagant was the Roxy Theatre in New York City, which modestly billed itself as "the Cathedral of the Motion Pictures." It had 6,214 red, plush seats and a 20-foot crystal chandelier. Uniformed ushers led patrons to their seats. For a few hours each week, any American—no matter how poor—could feel like they were royalty.

When the lights went down, moviegoers watched the best films Hollywood had to offer. These included lavish musicals by director Busby Berkeley, terrifying horror movies starring Boris Karloff as Frankenstein

Angels with Dirty Faces, *starring James Cagney, was one of several Hollywood gangster films that glamorized organized crime in the 1930s.*

and Bela Lugosi as Dracula, and fast-paced gangster films starring James Cagney and Edward G. Robinson. One of the most-talked about films of 1938—soon after Bugsy Siegel arrived in Hollywood—was the first feature-length animated movie made by Walt Disney. People thought Disney was mad to spend several years and 1.5 million dollars on a cartoon they felt could not hold an audiences' interest for 90 minutes. But when it was released, *Snow White and the Seven Dwarfs* was an instant classic. "So perfect is the illusion," wrote a reviewer in Variety, "so tender the romance and fantasy...that the film approaches real greatness." *Snow White* established Disney Studios as one of the most important studios in Hollywood.

A Celebrity Among Celebrities

Bugsy Siegel, top lieutenant in the national crime syndicate, was as much in awe of Hollywood's glamour and wealth as any starstruck kid. Upon his arrival, he rented a large house in swank Beverly Hills from opera star Lawrence Tibbetts. Siegel looked up his old pal George Raft, who was now a famous movie star. Raft introduced Siegel to many of the biggest names in Hollywood. They included actresses Jean Harlow and Norma Shearer and leading men Clark Gable and Gary Cooper. These celebrities found the good-looking, personable stranger from New York—who gambled recklessly at the race track and threw lavish parties—irresistible. They invited him to dinners and cocktail parties.

Although his long-suffering wife and two daughters had come to California with him, Siegel took every opportunity to enhance his reputation as a "ladies' man." His first conquest was the French actress Kitti Gallian. He is said to have spent $50,000 to get her film career going, but it was all in vain.

Siegel didn't just want to make someone else a star, however. He wanted to be one himself. He would go to the Warner Brothers studio and watch George Raft play scenes for his latest movie. Then Siegel would go back to Raft's dressing room and act out the same scenes himself that he'd seen Raft play. He worked hard to improve his diction. He even bought a 16-millimeter camera and had his old pal Moe Sedway film him acting. But all his efforts were for nothing. Siegel never got a call from a producer to be in a movie. The truth was, he was a lousy actor.

Organized Crime Comes to California

Even though Bugsy Siegel's movie career never took off, his career in crime flourished in California. Before Siegel's arrival, organized crime was all but non-existent in the Golden State. Local crime rackets had been run by small-time operators, like Los Angeles' boss Jack Dragna. The Mob sent Siegel to work with Dragna, who tolerated Siegel's interference but secretly looked for an opportunity to get rid of him.

Siegel quickly went to work improving existing rackets and creating new ones. He helped set up a smuggling network that brought heroin from Mexico into California. But his passion was gambling. He took over betting operations in Los Angeles horse racing, and he ran the off-shore gambling ships. His biggest moneymaker was the Trans America Wire Service, which communicated race results to bettors from around the country. Siegel offered the service to bookies (people who take bets) at a price that undercut the competition. Once he had the market cornered, Siegel suddenly raised prices for the wire service and demanded a cut from every bookie's profits. By 1942, the wire service was making millions for Siegel and the Syndicate.

Europe's Leading 'Gangsters'

While Bugsy Siegel was building a crime empire in southern California, more ruthless leaders were creating real empires in Europe. In Italy, Benito Mussolini was hailed as Il Duce, the Leader, by his people. Mussolini, who came to power in 1922, declared war on Ethiopia in 1935. It was the only independent kingdom left in Africa that had not been colonized by a European power. In a war that lasted less than two years, the Italians conquered Ethiopia and occupied it. That same year—1936—Mussolini made a pact with Adolf Hitler, leader of Germany.

Hitler had risen to power with his National Socialist German Workers Party, better known as the Nazi Party, by appealing to the same fascist, right-wing interests as Mussolini. A spellbinding speaker, Hitler promised the German people a bright future that would erase the national humiliation and economic depression that followed their defeat in World War I.

Further to the East, Josef Stalin, another ruthless dictator, was conducting a reign of terror in the Communist Soviet Union. In the mid-1930s, Stalin presided over a series of "purge" trials in which his

Benito Mussolini (left) and Adolf Hitler, tried to dominate the world in the 1930s and 1940s.

BUGSY SIEGEL AND THE POSTWAR BOOM

political enemies were accused of crimes and forced to confess under threats of torture to their families. In the summer of 1939, Stalin entered into a secret pact with Hitler. According to their agreement, Germany and the Soviet Union would not go to war with each other. Instead, they agreed to divide neighboring Poland between themselves. About a week later, German soldiers marched into Poland. The leaders of France and Great Britain, shocked by this act of aggression, declared war on Germany. World War II had begun.

Bugsy and the Countess

As war loomed over Europe, Bugsy Siegel somehow found himself caught up in these events. Siegel's latest girlfriend was the wealthy Countess Dorothy Dendice Taylor Di Frasso. The Countess was infatuated with Siegel and invited him to go to Italy with her in 1939. The trip was well timed. The newspaper, *The Los Angeles Examiner*, had just run a damaging exposé about Siegel's gangland connections. The story came as a shock to many of his Hollywood friends. It happened to be a good time for him to leave the country until things quieted down.

Soviet dictator, Josef Stalin, made a pact with Hitler that divided up Poland.

To help Siegel fit in with the European royalty they would be meeting, the Countess gave him a fake title. He was now Baron Bart Siegel, an English nobleman. Siegel, who was always trying to better himself in society, was undoubtedly pleased.

The European trip mixed business with pleasure. Both the Countess and Siegel were attracted to get-rich-quick schemes. Earlier, they had traveled to a small island off the coast of Central America in search of buried pirate treasure. They had found nothing but sand. Their latest scheme involved a powerful explosive called Atomite. Mussolini had expressed interest in the explosive, and the pair had visited him in Rome to demonstrate its destructive power. The sample of Atomite had failed to explode, and an angry Mussolini had demanded the return of $40,000 he had paid to develop the explosive.

About the same time they were in Rome, two of Hitler's top lieutenants, Hermann Göering and Joseph Göebbels, were also visiting Mussolini. The Nazis were already starting to systematically persecute Jews in Germany. Siegel, who was Jewish, took offense at this and later said he seriously considered shooting both men.

George Raft
～ Hollywood Star and Friend of Gangsters ～

A number of Hollywood stars reputedly owed their start to the patronage of gangsters, including Jean Harlow and Frank Sinatra. But few stars had as close ties to the Mob as George Raft. Raft grew up on the poverty-filled streets of Williamsburg, New York, and could have easily chosen a life of crime.

But Raft turned to show business instead. Once billed as the world's fastest Charleston dancer, Raft arrived in Hollywood at the end of the silent-film era. At first, his handsome looks landed him leading roles as a screen lover. But his New York accent and tough-guy manner soon won him leading roles in gangster movies. Perhaps his most memorable role was Guido Rinaldo, a coin-flipping gangster in the crime classic *Scarface* (1932), directed by Howard Hawks.

By the early 1940s, Raft's career was in decline. Much of this was due to his poor judgment in choosing roles. He turned down more good parts than any actor of his day, including detective Sam Spade in *The Maltese Falcon*, and Rick, the lovelorn hero of the 1942 classic *Casablanca*. Both parts went to Humphrey Bogart, and they helped rocket him to stardom.

Raft's friendship with gangsters like Bugsy Siegel hurt him when he turned to other business interests. He wanted to manage a London gambling club in the 1960s, but Great Britain refused to allow him into the country because of his Underworld connections. The United States government, meanwhile, went after him for unpaid back taxes. Despite his success in "high society," Raft remained a street-wise tough guy at heart. Near the end of his life, when asked about what happened to the $10 million he had made in the movies, Raft replied: "Part of the loot went for gambling, part for horses, and part for women. The rest I spent foolishly." It was a line that his old pal Bugsy would have appreciated.

Opposite: Actor George Raft, shown with actress Betty Grable, was a friend of Bugsy Siegel's.

Two Murders

If the Germans had put Bugsy Siegel in a murderous mood, he soon had the opportunity to indulge his desire. Upon his return to America in the summer of 1939, Siegel found out that Harry "Greenie" Greenburg, a minor Mob member, had been deported to his native Poland by the government as an illegal alien. But Greenburg had secretly returned to America and was hiding out in Los Angeles. He had sent word to the East Coast Mob that he would start talking to the police unless he was paid "hush" money to keep him quiet.

Word came from New York that Greenburg was to be eliminated. Al "Allie" Tannenbaum, a contract killer for Murder, Inc., was sent to Los Angeles to engineer the "hit." Siegel was only supposed to oversee the operation, but he insisted on being in on the actual murder of Greenburg. The others who were involved insisted that Siegel was too important to the organization to risk being part of a gangland slaying, but Siegel refused to listen. He was there the night Greenburg was riddled with bullets in front of his apartment. One of the killers, Whitey Krakower, unwisely began talking about Siegel's part in the killing upon his return east.

When news of this reached Siegel, he flew to Brooklyn and shot Krakower.

Bugsy Behind Bars

But Siegel and the Mob had a much bigger problem on their hands. Abe "Kid Twist" Reles, top lieutenant in Murder, Inc., was arrested back east. Fearing he would get the electric chair, Reles decided to turn informer. He began telling the police all about the inner workings of Murder, Inc. One of the many people he named was Bugsy Siegel. Based on Reles' testimony, Siegel was arrested and put in the Los Angeles County Jail to await trial.

Even behind bars, Siegel was a celebrity. He ate gourmet food, was treated like a king by guards and inmates alike, and had a free pass to leave the prison whenever he liked. By December 1940, all charges against him were dropped, and he was released. The District Attorney's Office felt that Siegel would prove a threat to Reles, and they needed Reles alive to testify against the even bigger bosses of the Syndicate.

Unfortunately, all their efforts were in vain. Sometime during the night of November 12, 1941,

Abe Reles' lifeless body was found on a landing six floors below his room in the Half Moon Hotel on Coney Island, where the authorities were keeping him. The party or parties who pushed him out his window were never identified. After that, Reles was known as "the canary who sang, but couldn't fly." Reles' testimony, however, was enough to bring down Murder, Inc. and many of its members. Louis (Lepke) Buchalter, the organization's leader, was arrested and later had the dubious honor of being one of the highest members of the Syndicate ever to go to the electric chair.

Chapter 4

"This morning was as delightful a Sunday morning as ever," wrote nurse Dorothea Taylor from Honolulu, Hawaii, on December 7, 1941. In a letter to her brother, she described that, "There was a cool breeze, for rain had fallen in the night....There was the sound of heavy firing in the distance as there so often is when our brave defenders are practicing....

When I stepped up to the street to look at the ocean, I noted heavy black smoke, as from oil rising from the region of Pearl Harbor."

The heavy black smoke was from sinking battleships, and the firing that nurse Taylor heard was from Japanese aircraft. The Japanese had launched a sneak attack on the Pacific Fleet that was anchored in Pearl Harbor.

Half the Pacific Fleet was wiped out in a few hours, and 2,400 American servicemen and women were killed. The following day the United States formally entered World War II, when it declared war on Japan.

Internment Camps in California

Hatred toward the Japanese for the Pearl Harbor attack spread quickly to the Japanese-American population, who had no connection to Japan. The vast majority of Japanese-Americans were hard-working, loyal citizens, but in the heat of war, many other Americans forgot this. In February 1942, President Roosevelt authorized the U.S. Army to force the evacuation of 120,000 Japanese-Americans—over half of whom were American citizens. They were sent by train to relocation or internment camps in remote,

In December 1941, President Franklin Roosevelt asked Congress to declare war on Japan.

desert regions of California, Arizona, and other western states. The detainees were treated little better than prisoners-of-war at these camps. Guards patrolled the camps night and day, and no one could leave. "We would play near barbed wire," recalls one camp resident who was a child at the time. "There was a target range not far from us. I can remember hunting around for bullet shells." Not until December, 1944, were these people, innocent of any crime, allowed to return to their homes.

Many Japanese-American families were sent to internment camps in California during the early 1940s.

BUGSY SIEGEL AND THE POSTWAR BOOM

Bugsy and Virginia

Bugsy Siegel's Trans America Wire Service was doing a booming business as the war heated up in Europe and the Pacific. Siegel now turned his attention to California's neighboring state of Nevada, where gambling was legal. Most of the serious gamblers went to Reno, the state's largest city in the north. Siegel was more interested in the dusty cowboy town of Las Vegas in the south, which was only a few hours' drive from Los Angeles.

About this time, Siegel met Virginia Hill, a petite, gray-eyed beauty with a strong personality to match his own. Unlike some of his previous California girl-friends, Hill was neither an actress (although she had appeared in a few films as an extra) nor an independently wealthy member of the Hollywood elite. She was a working girl, originally from Alabama. But the work she did was mostly Mob related. She was a courier for the Syndicate, sometimes carrying millions of dollars of mob money by train from Los Angeles to New York.

One wanted poster later referred to Hill as a "paramour and associate of gangsters and racketeers." She had been romanced by nearly every big gangster in the East, including an old Siegel pal, Joe Adonis. Men went crazy for her. One of her greatest admirers was Chicago gangster Al Capone's accountant, Joe Epstein, who sent her money regularly for years. "Once that girl is under your skin, it's a like a cancer," Epstein said. "It's incurable." In every way, the street-wise, high-living Hill was Bugsy Siegel's match. The two began a relationship that would last until Siegel's death.

The War at Home

While Siegel and Hill were carrying on their romance, much of the country was hard at work supporting the war. Eight million American women, teenagers, and older people went to work for the first time in their lives. With their husbands and boyfriends off fighting in Europe and the Pacific, women filled the work force, taking over every kind of job from riveting tanks and airplanes to shoveling coal. It was the first true taste of economic freedom for many women, and they relished it.

While industries boomed and workers had money in their pockets to spend on movies and nightclubs, food was in short supply. Most of what America

Millions of American women entered the workforce during World War II.

produced went to the servicemen and women overseas who consumed 20,000 tons of food a day.

What was left had to be rationed (given out on a
limited basis) to civilians at home. To conserve food
resources, Americans were encouraged to grow
their own vegetables in what were called "victory
gardens." By 1943, there were over 20 million such
gardens in every village, town, and city in America.
Wartime cookbooks included recipes that allowed
people to make the best of the food they had. They
included such specialties as a Wartime Cake made
without eggs, milk, or butter and a Civilian Defense

Americans were given ration books to conserve food during the war.

Cocktail composed of cold water, evaporated milk, and tomato juice. "…Waste," wrote the author of *Wartime Meals*, "is the unforgivable kitchen sin."

Lucky Luciano Does His Part

While Siegel and most other gangsters were too busy living in luxury to make any sacrifices for the war effort, one notable crime figure did play a significant role in the war.

HOLLYWOOD GOES TO WAR

"I don't want to go on imitating men, and that's all there is to it," said actor Sterling Hayden, as he prepared to enter the armed services. About one-sixth of the movie industry felt the same way and enlisted to fight in the war. Stars such as Jimmy Stewart and Clark Gable became fighter pilots.

Some leading men were rejected by the draft for physical problems. John Wayne had a bad shoulder, so instead of fighting on the front line he played the role of a soldier in numerous war films. Wayne was so convincing on the big screen, that some moviegoers believe to this day he was a real war hero.

Many stars discovered there were other ways to serve their country as entertainers. The USO (United States Organizations) put on over 420,000 live performances for the troops at home and overseas. American GIs (General Enlistees) laughed at comedian Bob Hope as he cracked jokes during his popular wartime shows. Others were treated to concerts by the Andrews Sisters, who performed their wartime novelty song "Boogie Woogie Bugle Boy."

Every entertainer from singer Bing Crosby to comedian Jerry Colonna used their talents and celebrity to sell war bonds. The money made from the sale of these bonds helped finance the war. Glamorous leading ladies, like Hedy Lamarr, sold kisses at special war bonds events for as high as $25,000 a kiss. By the end of the war, the public had bought a total of $36 billion in war bonds.

Americans were encouraged to buy war bonds to finance the war.

On November 9, 1942, the battleship *Normandie* mysteriously burned while it was docked in New York Harbor. Although it was never proved, many Americans felt it was an act of German sabotage. To tighten waterfront security, U.S. naval intelligence turned to—of all people—Lucky Luciano, who had been in prison since 1936. They knew Luciano still held power over the dock workers' unions, so they made a secret deal with him. If Luciano ordered the dock workers to be on guard for any sabotage of American ships at dock, they would commute (lessen) his sentence. Luciano accepted the deal, and there were no further acts of sabotage against ships in New York.

When the war ended, Thomas E. Dewey, who was now governor of New York, pardoned Luciano. "Luciano's aid to the Navy in the war was extensive and valuable," Dewey said. However, he was unable to win the gangster's complete freedom. Luciano was declared undesirable, and his American citizenship was revoked. He was deported to Italy, where he lived in splendor for 19 years, but always longed to return to the United States and his former prominence.

Charles "Lucky" Luciano (right, handcuffed to a prison guard) was deported to Italy in the late 1940s.

The War Winds Down

With the entry of American forces, the war was starting to turn against the Axis Powers of Germany, Italy, and Japan. In June, 1941, Hitler's troops invaded the Soviet Union, ending any possible alliance with Stalin. The Soviets soon joined the Allied forces (the United States, Great Britain, and other Western countries). Eventually, the Germans were driven out of the Soviet Union by the Red (Soviet) Army.

On June 6, 1944—D-Day—nearly three million American, British, and Canadian soldiers landed at Normandy beach in occupied France. It was the biggest land invasion in history. The Germans were slowly driven from France. On August 25, the Allies liberated Paris. Within six months, Allied troops crossed into German territory, moved east, and met the Soviets who were advancing from the west in April 1945. As April ended, Adolf Hitler was trapped in an underground bunker in Berlin, Germany. With few options left, he married his lover Eve Braun, and the couple committed suicide. Two days earlier, Mussolini, already ousted from power in Italy, was captured by anti-fascist Italians and was shot trying to escape.

Italian-Americans celebrated in the streets of New York City when Japan surrendered on August 14, 1945.

By May 1945, the war was over in Europe, but the Japanese continued to fight. On August 6 and 9, atomic bombs that had been secretly developed by the Americans were dropped on the Japanese cities of Hiroshima and Nagasaki. More than 130,000 people were killed. Japan surrendered to America five days later.

Of the more than 39 million people who died in World War II—including 12 million who died in concentration camps—only 274,000 were American servicemen and women. Europe lay in ruins, but America emerged from World War II stronger than ever.

A Ride in the Desert

One hot day, during that fateful summer of 1945, Bugsy Siegel invited his old pal Moe Sedway to take a ride with him. They drove from Los Angeles to Las Vegas to look at a few downtown gambling casinos that Siegel and the Mob controlled. Moe was puzzled, however, when his friend then took him to a lonely spot seven miles out of town where a ramshackle motel stood in the desert.

Siegel confided to his pal that he was about to build a hotel and casino on the site. It would be the most spectacular of its kind anywhere in the country. With Virginia Hill's help, he had even come up with a name for it—Ben Siegel's Flamingo. Flamingo was a nickname given to Hill years earlier. Moe must have looked at the flat, empty desert that stretched into the distance with a totally perplexed expression. He must have thought his old friend had been out in the hot Nevada sun too long.

Chapter 5

POSTWAR BOOM
A FLAMINGO IN THE DESERT

*A*ll his life, Bugsy Siegel wanted respect. It was the one thing he couldn't get with money, muscle, his good looks, or even his powerful personality. Sure, he could run the West Coast rackets, but he would still be working for the Syndicate back east. The Flamingo, the grand casino he dreamed about building in the Nevada desert, would be all his—or nearly. Billy Wilkerson, a Los Angeles club owner, first bought the property to develop it, but Bugsy came in as Wilkerson's partner and quickly took over a major share of the project. He eventually bought Wilkerson out.

Siegel, however, soon realized he didn't have enough money to complete his casino. The million dollars he had sunk into it wasn't enough. So he went to the Syndicate and got the mob bosses to invest another million. He had little trouble convincing his old partner Meyer Lansky to put in a share. Lansky saw gambling as a growth industry and had already built his own casinos in Miami, Florida, and Havana, Cuba.

Building a Dream

Construction of the Flamingo began in the spring of 1946 under the direction of top builder Del Webb. It wasn't the first casino built on what would come to be called the Las Vegas Strip. Two others—the El Rancho Vegas and the Last Frontier—were already there. But the Flamingo's bold architectural design would make it unique among Nevada casinos, most of which looked like Western gambling halls. Bugsy modeled the Flamingo after the elegant luxury hotels of Florida.

The El Rancho Vegas was a famous casino on the Las Vegas strip.

Its sweeping lines and hot pastel colors would conjure up a pleasurable oasis in the desert sands. The Flamingo would be, as *Las Vegas Life* called it, "the world's most lavish conception of hotel resort, casino, café, and playground all rolled into one."

With the nation just recovering from wartime rationing, building materials were scarce. But Siegel used his connections with the truckers' union and others to get the lumber, marble, and the other building supplies he needed. However, one of the nation's most successful criminals soon found himself being duped and robbed by his contractors.

"What made Bugsy a failure was that he was not a businessman," said Las Vegas talent agent Ed Becker. "He would bring in a ton of concrete today, and

BUGSY SIEGEL AND THE POSTWAR BOOM

when the sun went down they stole it and delivered it back again the next day…"

Siegel's gullibility was matched only by his extravagance. A plumbing bill for private sewage systems for 92 of the hotel's bedrooms came to a million dollars. Everything in the Flamingo had to be the best, which caused building costs to spiral out of control.

~ Pre-Vegas Nevada ~

Nevada had a reputation as a free-wheeling state long before Bugsy Siegel discovered Las Vegas. Gambling had been legal in Nevada since the 1800s, and divorce laws were loose compared to most Eastern states at the time. A "quickie divorce" in Reno required only a three-month residency. This gave out-of-state visitors plenty of time to spend their money on gambling and other amusements. Gambling was finally banned in Nevada in 1915 by reformers from the East. It was legalized again in 1931 when the mining industry collapsed, and the state had to find other ways to raise money. By this time people across America were saying "If you can't do it at home, go to Nevada."

Thousands heeded the call. Large casinos such as Harold's Club in Reno drew in locals and tourists alike. Billboards across the country beckoned motorists with the urgent message HAROLD'S CLUB OR BUST! By 1945, a year before the Flamingo was built, Nevada gambling was taking in nearly a billion dollars a year. With more money in people's pockets during the post-war boom, and restrictions lifted on travel after the war, Nevada gambling profits had nowhere to go but up.

The Rise of the Suburbs

While Siegel was building his dream resort, the rest of America also began a building spree. There had been no new home construction in the nation for nearly two decades, due to the Depression and World War II. Ex-GIs returning to the United States were marrying and starting families. In 1946 alone, more

After the war, many families moved to newly built suburban communities, such as Levittown, in New York.

BUGSY SIEGEL AND THE POSTWAR BOOM

than two million couples married, setting a record that would not be broken for 33 years. The next year, nearly four million babies were born. The post-war "baby boom" had begun. And all of these new families needed homes. The housing shortage was a serious problem.

Soon the demand for cheap, well-constructed houses was met by the Levitt family of New York. William Levitt, his father, and brother had a dream, but unlike Bugsy Siegel, they knew the construction business. The Levitts bought up 6,000 acres of potato fields on Long Island, 30 miles east of New York City. Next they planned a model suburban community for the site. They built small homes using the same mass assembly methods that wartime factories had used to make tanks and airplanes. The Levitts sent separate work crews to the building site. Each crew performed one of the 27 steps it took to complete one of their Cape Cod or ranch-style homes. At their peak, the builders were able to complete a house every fifteen minutes!

Each home in what came to be called Levittown, sold for a set price of $7,990. It was, according to a Levittown ad, "the housing buy of the century."

Young homebuyers agreed, especially when the down payment was small and the federal government guaranteed low-interest loans for veterans. Soon, new Levittowns sprang up in Pennsylvania, New Jersey, Illinois, Michigan, and as far away as Puerto Rico.

These suburban communities became a kind of paradise for young American families. The healthy, rural settings of these new towns were in sharp contrast to the cities, which were overcrowded and decaying from years of neglect. Urban crime was on the rise. So were racial tensions as thousands of African-Americans continued to migrate north from the South looking for job opportunities. War veterans also had vivid memories of the destroyed cities of war-torn Europe. If another war broke out closer to home, they didn't want to be living in a city.

The post-war housing boom was also a suburban boom, creating a new image of the "good life." That life included plenty of fresh air, safe streets for kids, backyard barbecues, and grassy lawns.

The New Bugsy

Just as America was making a fresh start, so was Bugsy Siegel. When his wife Esta sued for divorce,

Siegel complied and gave her $1.5 million in alimony. In the summer of 1946 Siegel flew to Mexico with Virginia Hill, where, she later claimed, they secretly married. With a new career and a new wife, Siegel was a new man.

But there was one change that he was most determined to make in his life. He made it clear that no one was to call him Bugsy ever again. "From now on it's 'Ben' or 'Benjamin,'" he told people. To improve his image, he hired a publicist and sent reporters cash and cases of liquor to write positive stories about him and his new casino.

As December 26, the official opening date for the Flamingo, drew closer, things started to go wrong. Randolph Hearst, the powerful head of the Hearst publishing empire, despised Siegel and refused to have anything good written about him in his newspapers. Studio bosses discouraged their stars from attending the opening, even though Bugsy had chartered a fleet of airplanes to fly them from Los Angeles for the gala event. Worst of all, the Flamingo's price tag had soared from $2 million to $6 million. Bugsy spent most of his waking hours borrowing money from friends and every mob boss

The Suburbs: Not Everyone's Paradise

While the growing post-War suburbs were a wonderful place to live for many Americans, two groups found it less than enchanting—African Americans and women.

Racial segregation was the unspoken rule in the first Levittown on Long Island, New York, and other suburbs followed its lead. Discrimination in housing was officially illegal, but realtors kept out potential black buyers by jacking up prices, offering them only the worst properties, and using other techniques. Soon these suburbs had a reputation for being unfriendly to minorities, which was enough to keep many African-Americans from even trying to find a home there.

If blacks were shut out from many suburban communities, many women found themselves shut in, virtual prisoners in this new paradise. Few suburban women at this time worked outside the home. They found what fulfillment they could in their husbands and children. Many families only had one car, and the husband drove off in it each morning to work. The wife was stuck at home, until her husband returned from work in the evening. Housework and childcare occupied much of a housewife's day. Ironically, although such new labor-saving appliances as dishwashers and clothes dryers made housework easier, many women spent more time on household chores than their mothers and grandmothers had 30 years earlier. They used housework to fill up the hours and avoid their worst enemy—boredom.

The better educated a woman was, the more likely she would experience boredom and frustration at home. Some educators went so far as to suggest women be banned from four-year colleges and universities because they wouldn't need an education. That way more classroom space would be freed up for use by men!

Levittown was the first model suburban community in America.

in America he could persuade to become an investor. He borrowed $100,000 from George Raft, which he never paid back.

As the opening date drew closer, workers labored feverishly, but the hotel was still unfinished. Siegel considered postponing the gala, but Virginia Hill wouldn't hear of it. Among other things, she had bought a $3,500 dress for the occasion and was determined she would get to wear it.

A Not-So Gala Opening

The day of the opening an artificial waterfall outside the hotel wouldn't work. On closer inspection, workers discovered a cat had a litter of kitten inside the top, and the animals were blocking the waterfall. Siegel refused to remove the kittens, thinking it would bring bad luck. But bad luck befell him, and the Flamingo opened anyway. A terrible rainstorm kept the planes grounded in Los Angeles and prevented those Hollywood celebrities who still planned to attend from

Actress Joan Crawford was one of the few Hollywood stars present for the Flamingo's grand opening.

making the trip. A few stars, including Clark Gable and Joan Crawford, managed to get to Las Vegas by car or train.

The opening night's entertainment was provided by George Raft, comedian Jimmy Durante, child star Rose Marie, and Xavier Cugat and his orchestra. "The show was spectacular," recalled Rose Marie 50 years later. "Everything was great, but no locals came. Las Vegas was cowboy hotels; this was Monaco [the gambling capital of Europe].... They were used to cowboy boots, not rhinestones."

Some locals did come, but only to look. "Everybody drove out Route 91 just to gape," wrote one journalist. "Such shapes!

On December 26, 1946, an unfinished Flamingo opened. Right away, the casino lost a lot of money, and Bugsy Siegel had to close it down.

POSTWAR BOOM: A FLAMINGO IN THE DESERT

Boomerang modern supports...and a scalloped swimming pool. Such colors! ...tangerine, broiling magenta, livid pink...Congo ruby, menthyl green...."

Inside the casino the atmosphere was equally exciting—but at the expense of the management. Customers won large amounts of money at the gambling tables, partly because some of the staff rigged the games so they could play and win too. Casino losses at the end of the week were a staggering $300,000.

The pressure to succeed was too much for Bugsy. He fought with everyone, even Hill. After one big fight, she left him and moved back to Los Angeles where she bought a new house. Bugsy kept the Flamingo open for a few more weeks and then wisely shut it down. He planned a grand reopening in March 1947 when the hotel would be finished.

One More Chance

The Syndicate back east was not pleased with the way the Flamingo project was going. The casino was losing money—their money. Frustrated and angry at his bad luck, Siegel refused to listen to the Mob when they asked for their money back. There were even rumors that he and Hill had taken some of the money meant for the Flamingo and put it away in secret Swiss bank accounts. Once again, Bugsy Siegel seemed out of control. This time, however, the Mob bosses were not prepared to put up with it.

At a meeting of the big bosses, someone suggested that Siegel should be "put to sleep" for mismanaging their money and possibly stealing some of it. Meyer Lansky spoke up for his old friend and partner. He urged the others to be a little more patient, to wait for the reopening and to see if business improved. He explained that the Flamingo could still be a success and make money for them all. The bosses reluctantly agreed to wait. Lansky's eloquent appeal actually saved his old friend's life. Siegel got another chance to make good. But this chance would be his last.

Chapter 6

If Bugsy Siegel felt his dreams of success were being thwarted, he wasn't alone. There was an underside to post-war America that was dark and disillusioning. Many of the returning GIs found the America they came home to was very different from the America they had left four years earlier. The pace of life was faster, and everything from food to clothing was more expensive. In 1946, Congress lifted wartime price and wage controls that had existed during the war. Prices soared. War production ended, and many people lost their jobs in the new peace-time economy, including nearly two million women. The men, no longer soldiers, returned to the workforce.

The men who had fought the war had changed, too. Combat experience had scarred some of them both physically and emotionally. For many veterans returning to civilian life was difficult. These issues were dramatized in such popular post-war films as director William Wyler's *The Best Years of Our Lives* (1946) in which three returning servicemen are beset by problems.

Like other young men and women, war veterans found life in the suburbs comfortable, but also strangely sterile. A growing feeling of rootlessness haunted suburban America. People who had lived all their lives in one place or neighborhood were now moving to new communities where they had to make new friends and live on blocks with complete strangers. Families were now more often separated as sons and daughters took jobs in growing companies that were sometimes located far from home in other states.

The Cold War

On an international level, there were new problems, too. World War II was over, but a new conflict was beginning to divide East and West. The alliance between the Soviet Union and the Western powers began to fall apart almost immediately after the end of the war. British Prime Minister Winston Churchill distrusted the motives of Soviet leader Josef Stalin in Eastern Europe. His distrust was justified. In 1946, Communist dictators trained in the Soviet Union took over the Eastern European nations of Bulgaria and Romania.

In March of that year, Churchill gave a speech in Fulton, Missouri, in which he declared "an Iron Curtain has descended across the continent" of Europe. This "Iron Curtain" soon fell over other neighbors of the Soviet Union—Hungary and Poland in 1947 and Czechoslovakia in 1948.

The Soviets' sphere of influence didn't stop in Eastern Europe. During the fall of 1946, Greek Communists, supported by the Soviet Union, rose up against the legitimate Greek government. By March 1947, U.S. President Harry Truman asked Congress for $400 million in aid for Greece and Turkey, which

Harry Truman was president from 1945–1953, a period that included the onset of the Cold War.

was also in danger of falling to the Communists. The money was approved, and it became the first action of what was known as the Truman Doctrine. According to this doctrine, the United States would help any free nation resist aggression from communism. Later that year, Secretary of State George C. Marshall proposed that the United States give economic aid to any European nation that would participate in its own recovery from the destruction of World War II. The Marshall Plan began the next year and helped millions of people living in European democracies get on their feet and resist the Soviets.

"Let us not be deceived," said American financier and presidential advisor Bernard Baruch. "Today we are in the midst of a cold war." Unlike previous wars that the United States had participated in, this war of words and propaganda would last for more than forty years.

The Flamingo Reopens

Bugsy Siegel could have used his own Marshall Plan, if only to pay back the Mob some of the $5 million he had borrowed to build his dream resort. But all he could do now was finish what he had started and hope it would be a success. All through February 1947, Siegel and his workers labored frantically to complete the hotel in time for the grand reopening of what he now optimistically called the Fabulous Flamingo. The schedule was so tight, that on the very evening of the reopening, Siegel and his friends were working side by side with the hired help to finish the bedrooms as the first guests waited to use them.

But the final product seemed well worth all the effort. Publisher Hank Greenspun wrote the following description in the magazine *Las Vegas Life*:

> *To capture its sweep and grandeur you have to be conditioned by a Goldwyn (Hollywood producer) set that's been dolled up by Orson Welles. This Flamingo is indeed a most colorful and amazing bird. Part of the plumage: 105 beautifully appointed hotel rooms, health club, gymnasiums, steam rooms, tennis, badminton, squash, and handball courts, stables with forty head of fine riding stock, a championship AAU specification swimming pool, a trapshooting range, nine hole golf course, nine different shops of national prominence....*

Everything in the Fabulous Flamingo was the best that money could buy. All employees, even the janitors, wore tuxedos. Table settings in the restaurant were sterling silver.

But in the weeks ahead, bad luck continued at Ben Siegel's gambling paradise. Guests were shocked when one hot day a swimming pool suddenly emptied. The water rushed down a crack in the pool caused by an engineering flaw. Siegel and Hill were back together again, but they were fighting more than ever. One day, Hill struck a waitress she believed Siegel was romancing, and the poor woman was sent to the hospital.

In 1947, the Flamingo reopened. The fabulous resort featured a swimming pool, restaurant, 105 hotel rooms, and a nine-hole golf course.

SHADOWS OVER SHANGRI-LA: A GANGSTER'S END

Seeing that business wasn't improving and that Siegel's life was in danger from the Mob, Hill tried to convince him to sell the jinxed casino and go with her to Europe where they would be safe. But Siegel refused to give up on his dream and clung to his gambler's hope that his luck would change. Soon, it did, and the Flamingo began to make a modest profit. But it may have been too little too late.

Last Night in Beverly Hills

Siegel spent the night of June 19, 1947, at Hill's luxurious Beverly Hills home on Linden Drive while she was in Europe. Some crime historians say his mood was upbeat. Others believe that he was resigned and emotionally exhausted. Earlier that day in Las Vegas, claims writer Colin Wilson, Siegel showed one of his underlings—Fat Irish Green—a briefcase containing $600,000. He asked Green to keep an eye on the case until "some guys come and take the money off your hands." Then Siegel left for Los Angeles. The next day, he met with his lawyers. He got a haircut and had lunch with friends. Later, he went to dinner at a seafood restaurant in Santa Monica and arrived back at Linden Drive that evening with his friend Al Smiley.

On June 19, 1947, Bugsy Siegel was shot to death at Virginia Hill's home.

Siegel sat downstairs on a flowered loveseat, reading *The Los Angeles Times* and chatting with Smiley in a room that looked out on the quiet street. Hill's brother Chick was upstairs with his girlfriend. Smiley later recounted what happened next. "All of a sudden there was this…racket, and then the world kinda blew up. There were shots everywhere, and glass was breaking. I ducked to the floor—then I heard more shots and more shattering glass. I didn't dare look up for a while, or find out what had happened to the others…."

Chick and the girl were untouched. But Bugsy was not so fortunate. Six steel-coated bullets from a 30-30 carbine rifle had shattered the picture window of the room he was in. Five of them had struck Siegel. In a matter of seconds, he was dead.

Twenty minutes after Siegel's death, Moe Sedway and Gus Greenbaum, another Mob associate, walked into the Flamingo and coolly told the manager on duty that the place was under new management. The Syndicate was taking over. It was as if Bugsy Siegel had never existed. Soon after, several businessmen came into the Flamingo and took the suitcase of money from Green, just like Siegel said they would.

Funeral for a Gangster

Bugsy Siegel's funeral was hardly the Hollywood event one might have expected. Only a handful of people who knew him attended—including his wife, two daughters, and a sister. Virginia Hill was in Paris. The Countess Di Frasso was also in Europe. George Raft was home suffering from asthma. The rest of the movie celebrities who had been his friends stayed away, afraid of bad publicity.

Bugsy was buried in a $5,000 silver-and-bronze coffin lined with silk. It was the last extravagance of an extravagant life.

"Bugsy" was gone, but the Flamingo lived on and eventually flourished. It was so successful that, within a few years, the Syndicate invested in the building of more casinos that featured the same outlandish elegance and spectacular entertainment. By the mid-1950s, the lonely desert highway where the Flamingo stood, now called the "Vegas Strip," was crowded with casino hotels. By 1991, the Flamingo had brought in over $100 billion in business. The dusty cowboy town on which Bugsy Siegel first pinned his dream had become the entertainment capital of the world.

IN THE SHADOWS OF FILM NOIR

A private detective is hired to track down the runaway girlfriend of a big-time gambler and falls hopelessly in love with her. A drifter goes to work in a restaurant, falls for the owner's wife, and agrees to help her murder her husband. A crazed gangster with an insane giggle shoves a woman in a wheelchair down a flight of stairs.

These plots are all taken from crime films that were released in 1946 and 1947. They have come to be called film noir, a name given to the highly stylized movies made in post-war Hollywood by French critics, which literally means "black or dark cinema." The "black" refers to the use of light and shadow in these films as well as the bleak and cynical outlook of many of the characters in them.

Because many film noir movies were low budget, B-pictures, stark shadows were first used to hide shoddy sets. But in the hands of imaginative cameramen and directors, the style soon became film noir's hallmark.

These films, according to writer Charles Hingham, picture "a world of darkness and violence, with a central figure whose motives are usually greed, lust, and ambition, whose world is filled with fear."

The world of film noir was inhabited by hard-boiled detectives, vicious gangsters, and beautiful but untrustworthy women. The settings were usually large, impersonal cities, such as New York or Los Angeles, and much of the action took place at night.

Among the leading actors who played in film noir movies were Humphrey Bogart, Barbara Stanwyck, and Joan Crawford. Some actors, such as Burt Lancaster, Kirk Douglas, and Robert Mitchum got the first big breaks of their carreers in film noir.

The style faded in the late 1950s but was rediscovered by young filmmakers in the 1980s and 1990s. Some of the movies they made were remakes of original film noirs, and others were new films. The theme of treachery and betrayal in a cold, unfeeling world still fascinates filmmakers and audiences today.

Opposite: Humphrey Bogart starred in many film noir masterpieces.

The Rest of the Story

Although she had stayed away from his funeral, Virginia Hill continued to love Bugsy Siegel long after his death. In 1951, as she was being questioned by a Senate committee investigating organized crime in America, a lawyer called Siegel "Bugsy." Hill exploded. "Don't you ever call Ben Siegel 'Bugsy,'" she cried. "I loved him. He was my man."

Hill eventually married a ski instructor half her age and had a child. But the marriage failed, and the Internal Revenue Service hounded her for years for unpaid taxes. One day in March 1966, the 49-year-old "Mistress to the Mob" took a handful of prescription pills near a waterfall in an Austrian village. She died of an overdose.

Other Siegel associates died of natural causes. Little Moe, who finally turned on his old pal, died in bed of several ailments. Lucky Luciano, still living in exile in Italy, suffered a fatal heart attack in the Naples airport in 1964. Shortly before his death, Siegel had met with Luciano in Havana, Cuba. Luciano had asked for his money back from the Flamingo, and Bugsy had given him the brush-off. That may have been Bugsy Siegel's death sentence.

In 1951, Virginia Hill testified in front of a Senate committee that was investigating organized crime in America.

Some people believe Meyer Lansky had Bugsy Siegel killed.

And what of Meyer Lansky, Siegel's oldest friend and partner? Did he have a hand in his death as well? For years, Lansky denied that he was involved in his friend's death. In an interview, writer Sidney Zion asked Lansky if he had given the go-ahead for Siegel's murder. "He was the best friend I ever had," Lansky replied. "His grandchildren are coming to visit me....How could I get a guy killed if I have his grandchildren coming to visit me?" "Lansky's eyes kept staring," Zion wrote. "That was when I knew that he had Siegel killed."

Meyer Lansky was forced to leave the United States in 1970 to avoid charges of tax evasion. He tried to enter Israel, but the Israeli government rejected him as an undesirable. Lansky tried to enter seven other countries, offering each a million dollars in cash, but they all refused. He finally returned to the United States in November 1972 and was arrested. But the charges against him didn't stick, and Lansky eventually returned to Miami Beach, where he died of lung cancer on January 15, 1983. He was 81 years old and was believed to be worth $300 million.

THE LAS VEGAS STRIP—POST BUGSY

The success of the Flamingo after Bugsy Siegel's death led other businessmen, often backed by Mob money, to build their own casino hotels on the three-mile-long Vegas Strip. Many establishments modeled themselves after the Flamingo's gaudy glamour and each tried to outdo the others in splendor and attractions.

The Stardust replaced the traditional entertainment of star comics and singers with a stage spectacular, the Lido de Paris, originally from France, that ran continuously for 31 years. The Riviera Hotel was the first high rise casino hotel on the Strip, rising to nine stories. In 1955, the Moulin Rouge became the first Strip attraction that welcomed blacks, who were often turned away from other casinos. It was declared a national historic site in 1992.

The first convention center came to the Strip in 1959 and included a vast exhibition area and a silver domed rotunda (circular room) that seated 6,300 people. It was replaced in 1990 by the 1.6 million-square-foot Las Vegas Convention Center, one of the largest single-level facilities in the world.

Today, the Strip is home to a growing number of mega-resorts meant to appeal to the entire family, not just high-rolling gamblers. These ambitious park-style theme resorts are modeled after circuses, pirate ships, and even a medieval castle. If Bugsy Siegel were to return to his beloved Vegas Strip today, he'd surely never recognize it!

In 1991, a Hollywood movie called *Bugsy* was released about the life of Bugsy Siegel. Handsome ladies' man Warren Beatty played the infamous gangster. Siegel would have been pleased by the casting, although he probably would have preferred to have played the part himself on the big screen.

Chronology

The Life of Bugsy Siegel

February 28, 1906	Benjamin Siegelbaum born in Williamsburg section of Brooklyn, New York.
1921	Forms the Bugs and Meyer Gang with friend Meyer Lansky.
1922–1929	The Gang grows and prospers selling bootlegged alcohol during Prohibition.
April 1931	Kills Mafia boss Joe Masseria in Coney Island restaurant with three other gunmen.
September 1931	Salvatore Marazano, last of old time bosses, is murdered by Lansky and Charlie "Lucky" Luciano gang; the modern Syndicate is born.
1934	Bugsy murders rival gangster Tony Fabrizzo while supposedly resting in the hospital.
1936	Luciano is convicted on charges of running a prostitution ring and is sentenced to 30–50 years in prison.
1937	Bugsy is sent to Los Angeles, California to oversee and develop the Syndicate's interests there.
1939	Travels to Europe with the Countess DiFrasso and meets Italian dictator Benito Mussolini.
1940	Arrested and jailed on testimony of Abe "Kid Twist" Reles; he is later released.
c. 1942	Begins a relationship with Mob courier Virginia Hill.
1946	Starts to build the Flamingo, a luxury hotel and casino in Las Vegas, Nevada.
December 26, 1946	The Flamingo's gala opening is a disaster due to bad weather and negative publicity.
March 1947	The Flamingo reopens with the hotel completed.

June 20, 1947	Siegel is shot to death by an unknown gunman at Virginia Hill's Beverly Hills home.
1997	The Flamingo celebrates its 50th anniversary as one of the first and most successful casino hotels in the world.

The Life of the Nation

1900	U.S. census declares that one-third of the population of New York City is foreign born.
1917	The United States enters World War I.
1919	Prohibition is enacted nationally, banning the manufacture and sale of alcoholic beverages.
1923	President Warren Harding dies suddenly; the Teapot Dome Scandal is exposed.
October 1929	The stock market crashes, leading to a severe national economic depression.
1933	Prohibition is repealed.
1939	Hitler invades Poland, setting off World War II.
December 7, 1941	The Japanese launch a surprise attack on the U.S. naval fleet at Pearl Harbor, Hawaii. The following day the United States declares war on Japan.
February 1942	President Roosevelt authorizes the U.S. Army to force evacuate 120,000 Japanese Americans to internment camps.
June 6, 1944	The Normandy Invasion by Allied troops on the north coast of France begins and proves to be a turning point of the war.
August 6 & 9, 1945	The U.S. drops atomic bombs over the Japanese cities of Hiroshima and Nagasaki; Japan surrenders five days later.
1946	Levittown, New York, the first model suburban community in America, is begun.

Glossary

bookies People who take bets on a horse race or other sporting event.

casino A building used for gambling.

commute Make less severe, such as a prison sentence.

contract An agreement; in the crime world, an agreement to kill someone for money.

extras Movie actors hired for minor roles, often without speaking lines.

film noir A type of crime or suspense movie characterized by a bleak and cynical outlook.

inquisitive Curious.

Mafia A secret organization that controls criminal activities.

newsreel A documentary film about current news events.

Prohibition Period of time (1920-1933) when the manufacture and sale of alcoholic beverages was banned nationwide.

pushcart A small, lightweight cart containing goods to sell that is pushed by its owner.

stool pigeon Slang word for a criminal who informs on other criminals to the police.

syndicate A large company or corporation, often used to refer to modern organized crime system first set up by Meyer Lansky and Charlie Luciano.

Source Notes

Chapter One

Page 6: "The Bugsy image was not something that was particularly endearing..." Mark Gribben. "Bugsy Siegel." Crime Library Web site. http://www.crimelibrary.com/gangsters/bugsy/bugsymain.htm

Page 8: "a map of the city..." Leslie Allen. *Liberty: The Statue and the American Dream.* New York: The Statue of Liberty-Ellis Island Foundation, 1985, p. 185.

Page 14: "Bugsy never hesitated when danger threatened..." Gribben.

Page 19: "He saw that a terrible death awaited them..." Frank M. Woolley. *The People's Almanac #2.* New York: Bantam Books, 1978, p. 534.

Chapter Two

Page 22: "Class, that's the only thing that counts..." Jay Robert Nash. *Bloodletters and Badmen: A Narrative Encyclopedia of American Criminals From the Pilgrims to the Present.* New York: M. Evans & Co., 1973, p. 502.

Page 23: "If they had become president and vice president..." Joshua B. Feder. *Gangsters: Portraits in Crime.* New York: Mallard Press, 1992, p. 30.

Page 24: "I don't know what to do..." Barbara Holland. *Hail to the Chiefs.* New York: Ballantine Books, 1990, p. 202.

Page 27: "The business of America is business." *The World Book Encyclopedia.* Chicago: World Book, Inc., 1986, Vol. 4, p. 815.

Page 28: "The streets were crammed with a mixed crowd..." Jon E. Lewis, ed. *The Permanent Book of the 20th Century.* New York: Carroll & Graf Publishers, Inc., 1994, p. 173.

Page 32: "We only kill each other." Nash, p. 504.

Page 36: "As time went on Bugsy became a little restless..." Gribbens.

Chapter Three

Page 40: "the Cathedral of the Motion Picture." *Discovering America's Past.* Pleasantville, NY: The Reader's Digest Association, 1993, p. 98.

Page 42: "So perfect is the illusion..." Leonard Maltin. *Of Mice and Magic: A History of American Animated Cartoons*. New York: New American Library, 1980, p. 57.

Page 51: "Part of the loot went for gambling..." Paw Prints Anecdotes Web site. http://www.geocities.com/Athens/Delphi/9910/raft.html

Page 54: "the canary who sang, but couldn't fly." Jason Fields. "Golden Age of New York's Mobsters." Daily News Online Web site. http:/www.mostnewyork.com/manual/news/mafia/mafia.htm

Chapter Four

Pages 55-56: "This morning was as delightful a Sunday morning as ever..." Lisa Grunwald and Stephen J. Adler, eds. *Letters of the Century*. New York: Dial Press, 1999, p. 267.

Page 58: "We would play near barbed wire..." Ibid., p. 57.

Page 59: "paramour and associate of gangsters and racketeers." Colin Wilson, ed. *Colin Wilson's World Famous Crimes*. New York: Carroll & Graf Publishers, Inc., 1995, p. 42.

Page 60: "Once that girl is under your skin..." Feder, p. 33.

Page 62: "...Waste is the unforgivable kitchen sin." *Discovering America's Past*, p. 49.

Page 63: "I don't want to go on imitating men..." *Decade of Triumph: The 40s*, p. 94.

Page 64: "Luciano's aid to the Navy in the war was extensive and valuable." Feder, p. 32.

Chapter Five

Page 72: "the world's most lavish concept..." Crimes and Punishment, Vol. 7. Westport, CT: H.S. Stuttman, 1994, Vol. , p. 860.

Page 72-73: "What made Bugsy a failure was that he was not a businessman..." Sidney Zion. *Loyalty and Betrayal: The Story of the American Mob*. San Francisco: Colliers, 1994, p. 90.

Page 73: "If you can't do it at home, go to Nevada." Dee Lillgard and Wayne Stoker. *Nevada*. Chicago: Children's Press, 1991.

Page 76: "the housing buy of the century." Alexander O. Boulton. "The Buy of the Century." *American Heritage*, July/August 1993, p. 63.

Page 77: "From now on it's 'Ben' or 'Benjamin.'" *Crimes and Punishment*, Vol. 7. p. 860.

Page 80: "The show was spectacular..." Gribben.

Chapter Six

Page 86: "an Iron Curtain has descended across the continent." *The World Book Encyclopedia*, Vol. 3, p. 425.

Page 88: "Let us not be deceived..." *Decade of Triumph*, p. 167.

Page 92: "some guys come and take the money off your hands." Wilson, p. 65.

Page 94: "All of a sudden there was this...racket..." *Crimes and Punishment*, Vol. 7, p. 859.

Page 96: "a world of darkness and violence..." Charles Higham and Joel Greenburg. *Hollywood in the Forties*. New York: A.S. Barnes & Co., 1968, p. 19.

Page 98: "Don't you ever call Ben Siegel `Bugsy'...." Hank Messick with Joseph L. Nellis. *The Private Lives of Public Enemies*. New York: Peter H. Wyden, Inc., 1973, p. 140.

Page 100: "He was the best friend I ever had...." Fields.

Further Reading

Brennan, Kristine. *Stock Market Crash of 1929* (Great Disasters). New York, NY: Chelsea House Publishers, 2000.

Claitor, Diana. *Outlaws, Mobsters, and Murderers.* New York: Mallard Press, 1991.

Cook, Fred J. *Mob, Inc.* New York: Franklin Watts, 1977.

Duden, Jane. *1940s Timelines.* New York: Crestwood House, 1989.

Editors of Time-Life Books. *Decade of Triumph: The 40s.* Alexandria, VA: Time-Life Books, 1999.

Feder, Joshua B. *Gangsters: Portraits in Crime.* New York: Mallard Press, 1992.

Joseph, Paul. *Warren G. Harding* (United States Presidents). Minneapolis, MN: Abdo Publishing Company, 2000.

Lord, Walter. *Day of Infamy.* Wordworth Military Library, 1999. (paperback)

Spies, Karen Bornemann. *Franklin D. Roosevelt* (United States Presidents). Springfield, NJ: Enslow Publishers, Inc., 1999.

Welch, Catherine A. *Children of the Relocation Camps* (Picture the American Past). Minneapolis, MN: Carolrhoda Books, 2000.

Web Sites

To find out more about the colorful, violent life of Bugsy Siegel, go to:
http:/www.crimelibrary.com/gangsters/bugsy/bugsymain.htm

For information on Murder, Inc. and other gangsters of New York's "Golden Age" of crime,
go to: http://www.mostnewyork.com/manual/news/mafia/mafia.htm

To find out more about Hollywood in its golden decades from the 1920s to the 1950s and see movie photo stills
and posters, go to: http://moderntimes.com/palace/welcome.htm

For eyewitness accounts of the Japanese attack on Pearl Harbor, try:
http://www.history.navy.mil./faqs/faq66-3.htm

To learn more about what it was like to live through World War II at home and see posters and other primary
source graphics, go to: http:/www.primarysources.org/curricula/artifacts/ww2

For various links on the history of suburbia in America, including family photographs of early residents of
Levittown go to: http://www.otal.umd.edu/~vg/msf 98/resource.htm#artifacts

Index

Photo Credits